G000320358

MANNERS
FOR
SCHOOLBOYS

MANNERS
FOR
SCHOOLBOYS

J. ROBINSON

THE BRITISH LIBRARY

First published in 1829 by Hamilton, Adams & Co. as
*A manual of manners; or, hints for the proper deportment
of school boys*

This edition published in 2015 by
The British Library
96 Euston Road
London NW1 2DB

British Library Cataloguing in Publication Data
A catalogue record for this book is available from the
British Library

ISBN 978 0 7123 5746 3

Cover by Rawshock Design
Text designed and typeset in Monotype Bodoni
by illuminati, Grosmont
Printed in Hong Kong by Great Wall Printing Co. Ltd

CONTENTS

———◆—◆—◆———

PREFACE

———•◆•———

THE DESIGN of this little compilation (for it pretends not to a much higher character) is to furnish school-boys with a text-book on behaviour, to which parents and preceptors may occasionally refer in their instructions and remarks on the subject of deportment. The compiler is aware it has been asserted that "Good breeding cannot be obtained from books;" that "nothing can make a young person thoroughly master of it but good company, observation and practice," and he is ready to admit that in manners as well as in morals, example is more powerful than precept; and that a genteel deportment in its highest polish, can only be acquired by associating with genteel people. Yet the science of good manners, as well as every other science, has a theory as well as a practice; and the one, must be considered, as preparatory to the other, and capable at least of illustration by books. Indeed, if books afford no assistance in the acquisition of a polite deportment, then some of our most celebrated writers have employed their pens in vain.

The compiler is not indeed acquainted with any work professedly on the subject, (hence the present attempt), except Lord Chesterfield's letters to his son; and these are perhaps too refined for school-boys; but there is a much stronger objection to them on the ground of their moral, or more properly speaking, their immoral tendency; on account of the gilded poison which they contain. "His Lordship," to use the words of Dr. Ash "has almost every where interwoven, art and cunning, flattery and dissimulation into his system of polite education. For this he is justly and highly reprehensible. There is not the least need that integrity and truth should be sacrificed to politeness and complaisance; and no design except a bad one can be served by such impotent and detestable accomplices as flattery, falsehood and prevarication."

"The worthiest characters" Dr. Fordyce very forcibly observes "are marked generally by an openness, and always by a probity, that reflects the greatest credit on their hearts, and on their understandings also. Yes, after all that a well known master, patron, and teacher has advanced to the contrary, I do not hesitate," he adds "to pronounce dissimulation, and indeed the whole family of cunning, by whatever name dignified, impotent and miserable apes of manly ability and genuine wisdom. Men of integrity and sentiment, display a nobleness which fails not sooner or later, to strike and persuade beyond all the paltry arts in the world, and I call" continues he " the best and greatest spirits of every age to witness that such men are placed on an eminence from which they may look down with superlative scorn on the whole race of knaves, liars and dissemblers."

These remarks are exceedingly applicable to the false and tinsel politeness of Lord Chesterfield, which tends to make men like whited sepulchres, fair and beautiful without, while within they are full of rottenness and corruption; but they by no means apply to that true and sterling politeness, which consists not merely in specious manners and a dissimulating address, but is founded on real worth and intrinsic virtue. Better indeed were it that the young mind should ever remain in its native rusticity, than purchase a factitious politeness at the expense of those nobler virtues which dignify mankind. This however is by no means necessary. Good nature is the essence of politeness without which art will make a very indifferent figure, and will in fact generally defeat its own ends. True politeness is that continual attention with which humanity inspires us, both to please others and to avoid giving them offence. The surly plain-dealer, who prides himself on his bluntness, exclaims loudly against this virtue, and prefers his own shocking rudeness and gothic freedom. The courtier and fawning sycophant on the contrary substitute in its place insipid compliments, cringings, and a jargon of unmeaning sentences. The one blames politeness because he takes it for a vice; and the others in a measure occasion this, because what they practice is really so. It must be admitted then that a truly polite deportment is a valuable acquisition and highly deserving the attention of young persons. Indeed a genteel behaviour is of the utmost consequence in private life, and may be considered as a passport to favour and fortune. It gives a polish and beauty to every other acquirement. Many persons even of inferior parts have been esteemed merely for their genteel carriage, while men of the greatest talents and learning have given disgust for the want of it. The celebrated Dr. Johnson from his boorish behaviour has been called the learned Hottentot; and perhaps more persons left his company offended at his rudeness than impressed with delight in his conversation and admiration of his splendid abilities. There is something which prepossesses us at first sight in favour of a well-bred man, and makes us wish to be like him: but there is certainly something still more captivating in an intelligent youth, who conducts himself with a modest dignity and suavity of manners equally remote from sheepish bashfulness and obtrusive boldness. On the contrary, how painful it is to be an observer of one of those lubberly boys, one of those premature aspirers to manhood, who is continually obtruding his booby remarks on the company in which he is suffered, correcting and contradicting his parents or any other persons, and every minute exposing his clownishness and folly. Nothing surely can be more disgusting and pitiable than this, except indeed that parental dotishness which can applaud as wit the impertinence it has cherished; which can admire as manly sense the stupidity it has nurtured.

It is desirable then that boys should be initiated betimes in the science of deportment, that they should be early instructed how to conduct themselves towards their superiors, their equals, and their inferiors; that they should be frequently taught how to behave with propriety under various circumstances; and that their minds should be frequently and deeply impressed with the importance of a correct and suitable demeanour. It is hoped the following pages will afford some useful hints and directions for these purposes.

The compiler respectfully leaves his little work to the candid consideration of Parents and Preceptors. His main object has been to inspire the youthful mind with chaste and honourable sentiments; and so far, he hopes, his humble efforts will prove not altogether unavailing.

PART I

BEHAVIOUR IN THE DIFFERENT RELATIONS OF LIFE

———◆———

I. KNOWLEDGE OF CONDITION AND BEHAVIOUR TO SUPERIORS

1. The first rule of wisdom is to know yourself.
2. "Know thyself," is one of the most useful and comprehensive precepts in the whole moral system. It is said to have been consecrated in letters of gold in the temple of Delphos.
3. In order then to know yourself properly, and to conduct yourself rightly, you must consider the situation and rank in life, in which Providence has placed you.

4. Reflect that under God you owe every thing to your parents, consequently you owe your first station in life to them.

5. For this you ought to revere them; and you are bound to regulate your conduct according to their condition.

6. The circumstance of your being sent to school, places you above numbers of indigent and vulgar children, who are suffered to wander about the streets; for this you ought to be grateful.

7. Be submissive to your preceptor: to him your parents have delegated their authority.

8. Be respectful to your teachers, and attentively listen to their instructions.

9. Manifest your sense of the privilege of being sent to school, by a zealous care and diligence in your studies.

10. Let your looks be complacent and composed: modest, yet confident. Frowning is considered a sign of an evil disposition. Regard with

attention whatever is spoken to you, and be ready with a proper reply.

11. Treat not the advice of your superiors with indifference, but let your actions testify that you highly value it; and let your looks as well as your words evince that your respect for them is sincere.

12. One of the most amiable traits in children, is their kindly receiving the advice of their parents and teachers; venture not on any thing of moment without proper advice. Do not receive it with reluctance; but invite it; implore it; cherish it.

13. You are too young to know always what is fitting for you, but your parents and teachers know and advise you for your good. They wish you to be preserved from every harm, and to be healthy, virtuous, and happy. By taking their advice you may be kept from many snares and dangers into which headstrong children will probably fall.

14. Be then always pliant and obliging; for

obstinacy is the offspring of ignorance and vulgarity, as pride and presumption are the parents of wickedness and folly.

15. Children who behave well, and always endeavour to follow the advice of their teachers, have seldom any reason to complain of their treatment.

16. It is the naughty, the careless, and the inattentive, who complain of the ill humour of their instructors; the fact is, they will not apply themselves to business, when it becomes necessary to find some method of punishment to make them more diligent and careful.

II. BEHAVIOUR TO EQUALS

1. Be kind and good-humoured to your equals and school-mates, and they will be kind to you; for kindness generally begets kindness in return.

2. Always speak to them respectfully; treat them

rather as superiors than the contrary; and you will meet with respect again.

3. Yet if any of them should be cross, still do you be civil, the churlishness of another will disgrace him; while your good nature will gain you love and esteem.

4. Always be ready to do a good natured act, and all who have any good nature, will be ready to oblige you.

5. Be mild, and gentle, and pleasantly familiar in all your words; and every one will desire your company.

6. Always endeavour to speak and act in the most unexceptionable manner possible; and never be ashamed of trying to be civil and to behave well.

7. By conducting yourself in this manner, you will obtain the esteem of your companions, and the approbation of your preceptor; you will be a comfort to your parents, and will moreover have the high honour of being proposed as an example to others.

III. BEHAVIOUR TO INFERIORS

1. If Providence has placed you in a condition above some other boys, this circumstance should not excite pride in you, but gratitude.
2. Avoid however any familiarity with such boys as are vulgar and uninformed; yet be courteous in all you say to them.
3. By no means treat with scorn or contempt persons that are beneath you in circumstance; such behaviour would set you much below them.
4. Think not every one your inferior who is not so well dressed, or who has not so much money as yourself: his talents may render him your equal, perhaps your superior; and talents and genius, if not degraded by misconduct, are always entitled to respect.
5. It is exceedingly rude to address servants in an impatient and hasty manner, as if you had no feeling, and considered them as devoid of it as yourself.

6. You should never address them in an austere, commanding tone; but whenever you want their services, accost them in a civil and obliging manner.

7. You should on no account deride the infirmities or incapacities of others; the strong should never despise the weak, for human nature is composed of such a delicate texture that it is liable to be rent in a moment; and those who to-day are possessed of the brightest parts, may to-morrow be reduced to a state of idiotism.

8. Avoid then all manner of haughtiness and insolence, if you would escape derision; and be affable and condescending to all. A scornful tongue and supercilious air will cause you to be disliked; whereas a kind and courteous behaviour will ensure you the love and esteem of all who know you.

IV. CONDUCT IN SCHOOL

1. Behave to your teachers with due submission, and treat your school-fellows with proper respect.
2. Do not run into the school, but advance decently and slowly to the door. On entering bow respectfully to your preceptor and walk directly to your seat.
3. Never talk unnecessarily in school; for talking interrupts your own business and diverts the attention of others.
4. If a stranger should come into the school, rise and bow as he passes you, and immediately attend to your book, not regarding that any one is present.
5. If you have any thing to say to your preceptor, wait until he is at leisure, and then speak to him distinctly and with respectful assurance.
6. When your preceptor speaks to you, rise and attentively listen to him; and look him modestly in the face, while he is speaking.

7. Begin not to answer until he has finished speaking; then, bowing respectfully, make a suitable reply.

8. Never dispute or quarrel with any one in school; such behaviour manifests, not only idleness but a bad disposition.

9. If a school-fellow gives you any annoyance, mildly desire him to desist; if he will not desist, rise up and waiting an opportunity when your preceptor's eye is upon you bow to him and state your complaint as briefly as possible.

10. On no account speak aloud in school; answer any questions, you may be asked, in a modest manner; distinctly and correctly repeat your lessons, when called upon to do so; and then observe a strict silence.

11. When a stranger is in the school do not stare at him; and when he is in conversation with your preceptor, or any of the teachers, do not listen to what is said; for that would be very rude and impertinent, and would evince that you neglect

your own business to mind what does not concern you.

12. Should the stranger address himself to you, rise instantly and attend to him; when he has concluded, bow, modestly look him in the face, and make a short and proper answer; and let both your manner and gestures be respectful.

13. Keep all your things in proper order, and preserve your books in neat and clean condition; and scrawl not over the leaves and covers of your books as some silly boys do, who as soon as they have acquired the valuable art of writing, thus ridiculously abuse it.

14. Diligently, carefully, and attentively pursue your studies; this will secure your improvement and procure you the love and esteem of your teachers and friends.

15. Some boys are prone to be dilatory; they put off every thing to the last moment; hence they are ever behind with their studies and business. Do not however defer *your* work, do not put off

to some *future* time what requires to be done *now*. When you have lessons to learn, or tasks to write, seize the first opportunity which occurs to perform them.

16. Let no desire you may feel, no persuasions from the idle, tempt you to delay the performance of your duty. When your tasks are done, your mind will be at ease, your play will be sweet, and your pleasures will be pure. Defer nothing then till to-morrow that can possibly be done to-day.

17. When school hours are over, quietly, softly, and decently depart out of school as you have been taught to enter: do not crowd or push to get to the door, this is unseemly, and shows an anxiety to escape from your studies.

18. Give time for those who are nearest the door to get out first; you cannot all go out at once, and by thrusting yourself forwards and filling the door-way, you defeat your own object.

19. In returning from school, go home without hurry and without delay: do not run as if you

were on some very urgent business, nor loiter as though time were of no value.

20. Never publish either at home or in any other place, what has been transacted in school: this is very improper; and a tale-bearer is universally despised.

21. Between school-hours endeavour to employ yourself in something useful; take great pains to improve. Too great a desire for play is unfavourable to learning. And let not sloth rob you of your time; for sloth like rust consumes more than labour wears; and a slothful boy will probably become an idle man.

22. There are many short intervals of the day, between school-hours and play, that may be, and that ought to be, turned to good account. Besides, idleness is the parent of want, vice, and misery. Would you gain fame, and wealth, and honour, when you grow up, you must prepare for the acquisition by gaining knowledge and habits of industry in your youth.

23. Reflect that play is not your business, but your relaxation when business is over; and think not that you have a right to be idle because you are young.

24. Look around you; all have business to perform, from the prince to the peasant. Consider the laborious ant, observe the industrious bee: all nature in fact is at work, all creatures are usefully employed, except the idle school-boy: his only business is his book, and that he neglects.

25. Reflect, that it is by youthful studies you must prepare for a useful manhood; and that industry promotes health, peace, and happiness.

V. DEPORTMENT
IN A PLACE OF WORSHIP

1. It is undoubtedly your duty to be respectful in school; but you are bound to behave with reverence in a place of worship; for there you

are more immediately in the presence of the Almighty.

2. Observe the utmost decency in approaching the House of God, and consider well whither you are going; that it is a place sacred to devotion.

3. Proceed slowly and quietly to the door; and on entering take off your hat. As you go to your seat, let not your eyes wander about; but walk steadily to your place.

4. When you have entered your pew, kneel down, cover your face, pray to God to keep your thoughts from wandering, and to enable you to worship Him in an acceptable manner.

5. Seat yourself where your parents, guardians, or teachers direct you, and remove not from *that* place until the service is over.

6. Observe to sit, stand, or kneel as the service requires, and conduct yourself reverently and devoutly as in the presence of your Maker.

7. Avoid even the appearance of irreverence in the House of God: do not loll and indulge yourself

in lazy attitudes, nor manifest a restless inattention, by gazing about you, frequently changing
postures, covering your face, or playing with
your handkerchief; but regulate your conduct
by the example of the best behaved and most
devout person in the place.

8. Look not particularly at any person during the
service; but keep your eyes modestly fixed on
the minister.

9. Converse not with any one during the time of
service, and endeavour to preserve your thoughts
as well as your eyes from wandering: attend to the
service with seriousness and devotion, and you
will find it both pleasant and profitable.

10. Let your mind and heart accompany the prayers;
they are offered to a pure and spiritual Being, to
a Being from whom we receive every good and
perfect gift: every comfort we enjoy comes from
Him, and He demands our grateful thanks.
Praise and thanksgiving indeed are the natural
expressions of a grateful heart.

11. Remember the text and listen attentively to the sermon; you are not required to get by rote the words of the preacher, but you should endeavour to retain the substance of his discourse.

12. The sermon explains and illustrates the scriptures, and enforces our duty to God and man; therefore attend diligently to this part of public devotion, and try to fix the truths inculcated in your memory: practice will render it easy, and you will thus increase in sacred knowledge, and perceive the excellency of that best of books, that most sacred of writings, the Holy Scriptures.

13. The Holy Bible is certainly the most beautiful, the most delightful of books. Written by good men inspired of God, it abounds with the most interesting relations. There we read of the great and good things God has done for us; there we learn how just, and wise, and powerful He is; and what we must do to please Him. There too we read of Christ, who suffered and died for us,

and who left us an example that we should follow his steps.

14. Indeed, the object of public devotion is not only to worship God, and to receive instruction, but that we may put in practice what we hear.

15. When service is over, covering your face, pray to God that what you have heard may be grafted in your heart; and that you may be enabled to bring forth the fruit of good living to the Honour and Glory of His Name.

16. Remain quietly in your place while others depart: do not hurry and crowd to get out; but when the way is free, decently retire, and return steadily home.

PART II

BEHAVIOUR AT HOME

———◆◆◆———

I. DEMEANOUR TO PARENTS

1. "Honour thy father and thy mother" is the command of God, to the observance of which the promise of long life, implying prosperity and every earthly blessing, is attached.

2. Whatever your parents direct you to do, if they are virtuous and good, you may be certain is for your welfare; therefore do it with cheerfulness and good will.

3. Nothing is more becoming in children than a prompt and cheerful obedience to parents or guardians; whereas obstinacy and disobedience are displeasing to both God and man.

4. If your parents chide or correct you, bear it with

meekness and humility. If you reply, let it be to acknowledge yourself sensible of your fault, and to declare that you will endeavour in future to avoid incurring their displeasure.

5. An undutiful or disrespectful answer would deservedly bring upon you additional punishment and disgrace; while a submissive and respectful one, if sincere, will assuredly procure you forgiveness and acceptance.

6. Should your parents at any time restrain you from doing what you have a wish to do, or prevent you going where you have a desire to go; bow submissively to their decision; they are much wiser than you are, and have most certainly your best interest at heart.

7. It is impossible for you to conceive the anxiety which your parents feel for your welfare: by day and by night, it is their study to make you happy; for you alone in fact they appear to exist.

8. They have taken care of you ever since you were born; in the period of helpless infancy when you

could neither move a step nor utter a word, nor do any thing but give trouble, they anxiously watched over you. They now supply all your wants; they provide for your education, they study your comfort; it is indeed their supreme delight to make you happy.

9. Ought you not then to make them every return in your power? Ought you not to treat them with the utmost reverence, in cheerfully obeying their commands, attentively listening to their advice, and carefully anticipating their wishes?

10. Return them, then, love for love; cultivate towards them the warmest affection; and remember that love is shown not merely by kind words and fair promises, but by steady and persevering acts of attention to their wants, deference to their wishes, and implicit obedience to their commands.

11. When in the room with your parents or relations, never privately steal out from them; for that is unhandsome; if you desire to go out,

ask permission, and if proper it will not be
denied you.

12. When strangers come in, rise, and after your
parents have paid their respects do you bow to
them. When you have bowed, continue a short
time standing; if your parents desire you to
sit down, do so, if not bow and retire from the
room.

II. CONDUCT IN FAMILY

1. On returning from school, go quietly up to the
door; scrape your shoes, walk directly into the
house, hang your hat in the proper place, and do
not touch it again till you go out.

2. When you go to school, bow, and bid your
friends "good morning" or "good afternoon;"
and salute them again on your return.

3. If you have brothers or sisters, it is your duty to
love them, to treat them with kindness and affection, and to do whatever you can to oblige them.

4. It is a delightful sight to see brothers and sisters mutually emulous to make one another happy.

5. On no account quarrel with your brothers or sisters; should any of them be cross or ill natured, still do you be mild, and gentle, and kind; and if that does not win them over, complain to your parents or relations.

6. Never revenge yourself; for this is wicked, your parents will always take your part if you behave yourself quietly.

7. Be courteous to servants; but not familiar with them; and do not hinder them at their work. Never speak haughtily to them, nor domineer over them.

8. Request them with civility to do what you wish to be done; and if they are good, and what you ask is proper, they will always readily do it.

9. Yet should they refuse to do what you request, you must not dispute with them; but complain to your parents, when, if you are in the right, they will see that your request is attended to.

10. Be not however too forward in making complaints, else neither the servants nor your parents will regard you.

11. Be not noisy in the house or you will disturb the family; noise and rudeness are marks of disorderly children. Beat your drum and whip your top out of doors, and run, and jump, and talk aloud in the fields; yet not so as to annoy any one even there; but in the house and among your friends, be quiet and sedate.

12. If you have permission to play, do it without noise: orderly children know how to amuse and divert themselves without disturbing the peace of others.

13. Whatever be your condition, be moderate in your dress: covet nothing but what your parents can afford. A desire for showy finery indicates a common mind.

14. Wear not your best things on common occasions; dress according to your employment, time and place. Be very careful of your clothes;

let them not lie about to get soiled, but put them into your drawers; this habit of order will be ever valuable; it will save time and trouble; it will prevent loss and vexation, and you will be able to appear more creditable and decent at a less expense.

III. BEHAVIOUR AT MEALS

1. Nothing perhaps shews more strikingly the difference between vulgar and well bred boys, than their respective behaviour at meals.
2. Learn the time of dinner and always be ready a quarter of an hour before it is served. Never come to the table heated or in a hurry; but be in the room clean washed, and combed, and dressed before the company enter.
3. When grace is about to be said, advance to the lower end of the table, the end opposite that at which the mistress of the house sits, wait till

every one is seated, and then take the place appointed you.

4. Wait patiently till the company are served; never attempt to help yourself nor to ask for any thing till you see the company are all helped, when if it happen that you have been forgotten, you may modestly request to be served.

5. Be satisfied with whatever is given you, nor wish to exchange it for something else, and always eat with decency and cleanliness.

6. When dining abroad, should the master or mistress of the table offer you any thing; to pass it to the person next to you would be to charge him or her with the want of good manners, or of a proper respect to the company, and especially should you be the only stranger present; and should any thing in particular be offered to you, unless you have a dislike to it, it would be rudeness to refuse it, with ever so genteel an apology.

7. If you want any thing of the servants, wait till

they are at leisure; and never call them when they are attending on some other person.

8. Use your knife and fork, and touch no part of your food except your bread or a bone with your fingers; to touch the food of any other person, even the bread, is extremely rude.

9. Cut, or break your bread; it is very vulgar to bite or gnaw it; and place it to the left of your plate.

10. Eat not greedily, thrusting your food into your mouth with both hands as if afraid of losing time; nor eat large mouthfuls, nor seem anxious to have the most of any particular dish.

11. Do not hold your knife and fork with the points upwards; or dip your fingers, or any thing you have tasted into the sauce; or make a munching, smacking noise in eating; or lick your fingers, knife, or plate; these are all extremely vulgar and disgusting habits.

12. Do not loiter over your victuals, or keep your plate when others have done; nor yet be impatient to be gone; quit not your seat till the table

be dismissed; and keep your eyes upon your own plate, and suffer them not to stray upon the dishes, or upon the plates of any one in company, as if you longed for their food, or for something you have not.

13. Wipe your mouth frequently while you are eating, and lay your knife and fork on your plate, lest you soil the table cloth.

14. Take salt with the salt spoon, or with a clean knife; never use for this purpose the one with which you are eating, as that would foul the rest.

15. Sit upright in your chair, and do not loll or lean against the table. Incline your body a little as you take in your food; but do not hover over your plate or the table like a hawk over his prey, spreading out your arms and thrusting your elbows in the faces, or on the plates of those who sit next to you.

16. Present not to others what you have tasted, nor eat what other persons have left; both these acts are indelicate.

17. Do not find fault with any thing at table, nor yet immoderately praise it; and by no means smell to any dish as if you suspected its being unwholesome.

18. Do not laugh at table, much less sneeze, or cough, or yawn; yet if you are unavoidably seized with a fit of sneezing or coughing, hold the napkin, tablecloth, or your handkerchief before your face, and turn your head aside from the table.

19. If what is given you be too hot, wait patiently for its cooling, lest you spirt it all over the table; and always chew your food properly before you swallow it; but do not distort your countenance, or make a wry face during the process; and swallow one mouthful before you take another.

20. Should any thing hurt your mouth, or should a bone stick between your teeth, hold up the napkin or your handkerchief with your left hand while you remove it with the other.

21. Do not pick your teeth with a fork, or thrust

your fingers into your mouth; or put a spoon which you have used into the dish or tureen.

22. Pick bones clean and leave them on your plate, and do not throw them on the floor or give them to dogs; and do not handle dogs or play with them while at dinner.

23. In eating fruit do not swallow the stones; but lay them and the stalks on one side of your plate, putting one of the leaves which came with the fruit over them.

24. Empty your mouth entirely and wipe it before you drink, and do not put the cup or glass far into your mouth, or cough in it, or drink too greedily or too long, till like a horse you are forced to breathe in your draught; and do not blow or breathe into another person's cup, or glass, or over his plate.

25. With respect to drinking healths, follow the custom of the company in which you happen to be; copying in this as in all other matters

relative to behaviour, the example of the most accomplished person at table.

26. Always empty your mouth and wipe it clean before you speak, and never indulge in any indelicate, unseemly or impertinent discourse.

27. Be particularly careful not to spill soup, or gravy, or sauce of any kind upon either your own garments or those of any other person.

PART III

DEPORTMENT
IN COMPANY

———•◆•———

I. CONDUCT WITH COMPANY
IN THE HOUSE

1. When you first enter a room in which there
   is company make a graceful bow; sit in a
   genteel and easy posture; do not stretch out
   your legs, loll or put yourself into any unseemly
   attitude.

2. Do nothing to offend any one's sense or
   imagination; exhibit nothing in company of a
   disgusting nature.

3. Observe the greatest cleanliness both in
   your person and apparel; and particularly
   avoid belching, biting or cutting your nails,

47

scratching your head, rubbing your teeth, and picking your nose and ears in company.

4. Sing not or whistle to yourself; nor drum on the table, nor kick your chair or the floor; nor grind or gnash your teeth; nor scrape or make any other sound or noise which however amusing to yourself must interrupt and annoy others.

5. Make no wanton, waving, or swinging motions, and when you stand, whether you are speaking or silent, stand still and at ease.

6. Do not spit, or cough, or sneeze except when unavoidable, and then turn your head aside from the company and hold up your handker-chief; and both in coughing and sneezing make as little noise as possible.

7. Never yawn in company; for it is a bad compli-ment to those present, and looks as if you were weary of being with them: endeavour to conquer a disposition to do so; yet if you cannot conquer it turn your head aside and hold up your handkerchief.

8. Seldom blow your nose in company, and always use your own handkerchief; never ask the loan of another person's nor offer yours to any one: and do not like Chesterfield's clown look into your handkerchief when you have used it: in blowing your nose too, make as little noise as possible.

9. Do not wink or distort your face, or shrug up your shoulders; do not shake your head, or rub your elbows or knees; these are all ridiculous tricks, which, if persevered in, will become habitual and expose you to be laughed at.

10. Do not crowd towards the fire or thrust yourself forward to the best or highest place; at the same time be not troublesome by impertinently debasing yourself, by refusing to go first or take a particular seat, throwing your arms about like a fencer, and spending time and giving trouble to be intreated to do what all the while you desire to do, or what is proper you should do.

11. Should the master of the house or a superior

direct you to a seat, take it immediately without any apology.

12. Never sit with your back on any one, or lean upon another person's chair: do not look over a person who is reading or writing, nor into books and papers which lie about.

13. It is very rude to endeavour to partake of another person's secrets: whether letters, discourses or writings of any kind, unless you are particularly requested to do so; and then you should keep sacred the confidence reposed in you.

14. If any thing be given to another person to read, take it not out of his hand, nor be hasty to be first to see any curiosity, or be anxious to know what any one is doing or studying.

15. Do not read in company except if you are requested to do so; and if a letter is delivered to you which requires your immediate attention, apologize, or request permission to retire a few minutes.

16. Never whisper in company, nor laugh except the occasion of your laughter is evident to all: for some one might suspect himself to be the subject of your whispering or mirth.

17. If you have any particular or private business with any person, retire, or take him aside, after you have asked leave to do so, and when no one is discoursing, and while you talk thus privately look not particularly at any one.

18. Whenever there is occasion for you to laugh let it be done moderately, not with the boisterous horse laugh of the clown.

19. Should any person in company have a particular infirmity, or singular features, or any thing remarkable about him, it would be very rude to be seen to notice it; much more to make it the subject of conversation or inquiry.

20. Be at all times particularly attentive to the female part of the company; wait upon the ladies on all occasions; pick up with alacrity every thing they drop, be very assiduous in procuring

them whatever they want; be blind to what you should not see, and deaf to what you ought not to hear.

21. Opportunities of shewing these little attentions are continually presenting themselves; and where they do not you must study to create them.

22. Never frown, but always look contented, cheerful, and complacent, in company: do nothing that resembles superiority, nor usurp upon their rights; nor do any thing by which any one present may think you do not love, prize, or respect him.

23. Should you at any time have a message to deliver from your parents or friends; do not in delivering it hang down your head, play with your fingers, or mumble so that you cannot be understood; but stand erect, assume a modest confidence and speak distinctly, correctly, and gracefully.

24. A sheepish shamefacedness in company is

perfectly ridiculous; shame should accompany only bad actions, not those which are praiseworthy.

25. To pay proper compliments to those to whom they are due can never be a just cause of shame, though to omit paying them might indeed cause you to blush.

26. Endeavour then to overcome this foolish, misplaced shame, and never, while you are sensible you are doing what is right and proper, let false bashfulness make you feel awkward and uneasy.

27. Always summon sufficient resolution to speak with propriety when spoken to, and modestly pay civility to every one.

28. Always be cheerful and good humoured without being troublesome, silly, or noisy; be obliging and complaisant without the least degree of affectation, and use every effort to overcome that ridiculous bashfulness which never is productive of any good, and which differs almost as widely from true modesty as light does from darkness.

29. In going out of a room be sure not to bang the door after you, but shut it gently so as to make the least possible noise and disturbance.

30. In short, at all times and in all companies, pay a proper regard to your exterior carriage and behaviour, since without that attention every expence bestowed upon your education will in a great measure be thrown away, and the more material good qualities you possess be so obscured, as in the eyes of the world to lose all their lustre, and consequently will not be of half the service they otherwise would be.

II. CONVERSATION

1. Always look in the face of the person with whom you are conversing, but do it modestly and decently.

2. Let your looks be pleasant and composed; modest yet confident; but gaze not upon any one as if you were taking his portrait.

3. Modesty is more graceful than boldness, boldness than bashfulness, and bashfulness than impudence. Some persons know not how to look, but think they do best when they are most extravagant.

4. Fix not your eyes constantly upon one object, for that denotes amazement or absence of mind. Wandering and inconstant looks express unsettled thoughts; winking is the act of light mindedness; and putting the hands in the pockets denotes neglect and self importance.

5. Let not your mouth approach so near to the person you are conversing with as to bedew him, or in any way offend him with your breath.

6. It is rude in any person to engross all the conversation to himself: young persons particularly should never be too forward when in company with persons older than themselves. "Listen and learn" should be your maxim. Wait till you are spoken to, or till your opinion is asked on any subject, and then let your answer be distinct,

modest and brief. Your good sense in fact must inform you when it is proper to speak and when to be silent, and let it be your constant endeavour to please and oblige every one.

7. Answer no one till he has spoken; for those who are impatient to hear are generally rash to censure; and do not turn your back upon or correct the speaker: depart not before he has done, and prevent him not by helping him out with what he seems to have forgotten.

8. Do not exclaim when a story is related or any thing said, "I have heard this before, I knew it already." Accept what is said as new and in good part.

9. Tell not what happens to come into your fancy in the midst of another's discourse, nor anticipate what he would say; if however it be proper to interpose, do it not without asking leave, else you will impede conversation and occasion misinterpretations; whence arise arguings without conviction, and tattling to no purpose.

10. Be not magisterial in your dictates, or dogmatical in your assertions: contend not pertinaciously in common discourse for your opinion, nor even for a truth of small consequence.

11. Declare your reasons, and if they are not accepted, assure yourself that you are not obliged to convert the whole world to your opinions.

12. Be not forward in censuring or contradicting any one; but always be ready to cede your point to the general sense of the company. You are not obliged to encounter every thing which you disapprove, to confute all that you conceive to be false, nor to formalize upon all the foolery and nonsense you may chance to hear. There is no need for you to set up as a universal reformer.

13. In a controversy, say not all that may be said; but only what appears to be really necessary.

14. After you have related a story or fact that appears somewhat incredible, do not swear to it, nor use any imprecations on yourself, nor lay a wager, nor fancy yourself engaged to defend it,

nor suppose that every one who does not seem
to give implicit credence to it intends to affront
you.

15. Repeat not frequently the same thing, and be
not impatient for the company to listen to you:
leave them at liberty, and imagine the fault to be
yours that you do not command attention.

16. When a story has been related in your presence,
ask not what has been said, nor desire to have it
repeated, for that would evince your contempt
of the relater, in your minding not what was
spoken, and in desiring him to tell a tale as
often as you chuse to ask it.

17. Yet should it happen at any time that you do not
understand what is said to you, do not exclaim
what! hey! what do you say! as vulgar boys do,
but say *sir!* or *madam!* and respectfully apolo-
gizing for your inattention and the trouble you
are giving, politely request a repetition of what
has been addressed to you.

18. Do not strike, or pinch, or pull, any person to

attract his attention: do not talk of yourself, your family, your horses, your dogs &c. and tell not your dreams, when perhaps your waking thoughts are not worth reciting.

19. Use not commonly or unnecessarily the name of God, nor that of the devil, nor lightly quote passages of Holy Scripture in conversation. And do not mock at or ridicule holy persons, things or actions; for such conduct is not only indecent, but sinful; and practised only by persons devoid alike of religion and good sense.

20. Swearing is a vice which has no temptation to plead: it affords no gratification, and is as vulgar as it is wicked.

21. Never on any pretence be guilty of telling lies, or romancing, as it is called, in conversation. Remember, as long as you live, that nothing but strict truth can carry you through life with honour and credit.

22. Truth is the basis of every virtue: it is the voice of reason and of nature, and possesses the most

powerful charms. Every deviation from truth, however trifling, is criminal; religiously then obey its precepts, never transgress its limits. Let no fear of shame, no motives of gain, no dread of pain, induce you to violate it on any occasion.

23. Truth stamps a merit on the youth who adheres to it; but lying is an odious vice, an abominable practice. Dread then the utterance of an untruth; if you do not, you will lose your good name and character, and will be deservedly shunned and despised.

24. Liars are not only disagreeable companions, they are really dangerous ones: they carry a moral contagion about them, and when known will ever be avoided by persons of sense, understanding, and integrity.

25. The person who tells lies, uses indecent expressions, or swears in company, be his rank, fortune and profession what it may, is an abandoned character, and justly despised by all truly genteel and well-bred people.

26. Speak not through the nose, nor with any affected or unhandsome gesture, such as distorting the mouth, swelling the cheeks, and the like. If you have not a pleasing pronunciation, endeavour to recompence the defect by the excellence of the matter which you introduce into conversation.

27. Interrupt not your own discourse or that of others by coughing, hemming, or any disagreeable noise. A little well-timed laughter may be permitted, and graceful smiling commended; but never laugh at your own jests, stories, or sallies of wit and humour.

28. In answering a question in the affirmative or negative, do not say bluntly *yes*, or *no;* but *yes, Sir,* or *no, Sir; yes, Madam,* or *no, Madam;* according to the rank and sex of the person you are addressing.

29. Address every person by his proper and most distinguished title, and shew that particular respect to him which his office, character, or station, may seem to require.

30. A failure or blunder of this kind may intend no disrespect to the person to whom the address is made, but it will always be considered as a mark of ignorance, inattention or ill manners, in him that makes it; therefore for your own sake endeavour to avoid it.

31. If you were speaking to the king or queen, you should say, *your Majesty*; if to a prince or princess, *your Royal Highness;* if to a duke or duchess, *your Grace;* if to a lord or lady, *your Lordship* or *Ladyship;* if to a commoner, *Sir* or *Madam*; if to your servant, *John* or *Mary*, or whatever his or her name may be.

32. And observe, that though it is the custom of the country thus to distinguish people of different ranks by different epithets, yet politeness, civility, affability, and good-humour are due to all; and you should no more suffer yourself to speak rudely to your servants than to your superiors.

33. Accommodate as much as possible, the subject of your conversation, as well as the manner

of your address, to the different ages and circumstances of the persons with whom you converse.

34. If you are not understood, blame yourself that you either speak not clearly or that you do not accommodate yourself to your hearers.

35. Esteem the faults you commit against others to be great, that you may avoid them; those of others against you to be small, that you may excuse them.

36. Of all things, beware of sullenness, melancholy, and ill humoured silence; as if you observed and censured what every one did and spoke. Yet silence perhaps in a studious person may be tolerated. If something excite the laughter of the company, it would be ridiculous to assume the ill-timed gravity of the judge.

37. Yet to be complaisant in conversation, it is not necessary that you should echo what every one says, or that you should do whatever you see another person do; that you should merely make

up a number and sit like an automaton in the company.

38. To acquiesce with every thing is as bad, or perhaps worse, than to comply with nothing; as much as contempt is below hatred.

39. He that is truly polite knows how to contradict with respect, and to please without adulation. The manners of a well bred person are equally remote from insipid complaisance and low familiarity.

40. Discover by your attention and manner that you wish to profit by the observation and experience of all whose good sense, reputation, and knowledge of the world, may be thought to afford you the opportunity of doing it.

41. Be affable and condescending: never so much as seem to think yourself above speaking to the meanest of the company in which you happen to be; address yourself to all as occasion may offer, and attend instantly to every one who speaks to you.

42. Pride, insolence, stateliness, imperiousness and anger, are not signs or qualifications of gentlemen; but the scandal of conversation; and proceed from a spirit of presumption, from a want of breeding, which conceives itself to be above others, which thinks itself wiser and better than they are; and which prompts a person to imagine that he alone ought to be the rule to which others should conform; that all others are wandering stars, himself only in the Ecliptic.

43. The conversation of all persons is not equally elegant and engaging; yet it would be exceedingly rude not to listen to an individual whose qualifications are not of the first rate in this respect, and by a marked inattention to tell him in language sufficiently plain, that you think him a blockhead and not worth the hearing.

III. DEMEANOUR IN COMPANY
WHEN WALKING ABROAD

1. When you are in company, walking abroad,
   behave to them with the same respect which you
   have been instructed to do when at home, or in
   the house.
2. Turn your face towards the company, particularly to ladies, or to your superiors when
   they speak to you, or you to them: be attentive
   to their remarks, and walk along quietly and
   decently.
3. Should any one in company in passing an acquaintance bow to him, do you bow too, though
   you do not know him: this is a respect you owe to
   your friends.
4. Should you meet an intimate, do not stop to
   converse with him, this would be rude.
5. In crossing a street let the company go first;
   yet should a superior request you to go on, or to
   enter a carriage before him, it would be contrary

to good breeding to draw back or to hesitate a moment.

6. Should you see any thing which particularly attracts your attention, do not stop to stare at it, but give a passing look and go on.

7. Never on any account run far before, or stay any distance behind, your company.

IV. CONDUCT IN WALKING ALONE

1. Pay a due respect to yourself when alone, and walk as decently as if you were in company.

2. Do not whistle, sing, or shout, or make any silly noise as you walk along: these are marks of rudeness and folly.

3. Walk a steady, genteel pace, avoiding the affected strut of the coxcomb, as well as the awkward waddle of the bumpkin.

4. Behave with proper respect to all you meet, and to all you pass in your walk: insult not, or molest a boy that is less or weaker than yourself; and by

no means cast a reflection on any one afflicted with personal infirmities; but be thankful that the case is not yours.

5. Treat your seniors and superiors with a becoming respect, always giving them the wall; and if you meet them in a narrow way, give them all the room to pass you possibly can.

6. Bow gracefully to those you know when you meet them or pass them, and take off your hat when any nobleman or great personage passes you, though you do not particularly know him: it is a respect due to his rank.

7. When a superior meets you and speaks to you, take off your hat while you answer him; and stand respectfully without it till he leaves you, unless told to put it on.

8. Run not in the way of such as are passing, nor stare in or listen at the windows or doors of houses as you go along a street; nor wish to overhear the discourse of persons as you pass them: this is very rude.

9. When you come near a mob of persons, walk to the other side of the street, and concern not yourself about the matter or circumstance which collected them together.

10. Should you in your walk meet a rude or unmannerly boy, give him the way; you should no more dispute or hold any altercation with him than you should keep him company.

11. Repeat not vulgar jests against any person, nor give or use a nickname to any one; such vulgarities are more disgraceful to those who practice them, than to the individuals who are the subject of them.

12. Do not hop, and skip, and jump instead of walking; and throw not your arms about, or use any other antic motions. Observe how genteel and well-bred persons walk along; and endeavour to walk like them.

PART IV

KEEPING COMPANY

———◆◆◆———

I. OF ASSOCIATING WITH OTHER BOYS

1. Chuse for your companions and intimates the most decent and genteel, and the best tempered, amongst your school-fellows; avoiding any intimacy whatever with such as are clownish, dirty, impudent or cruel.

2. There are certainly too many children, who from want of proper care in their education, are frequently guilty of little, disagreeable, illiberal tricks, and who accustom themselves to many words and expressions which are easily learned, though very improper to be used; hence the necessity of being careful with whom you associate.

3. Engage in no play that may expose yourself or your companions to danger: avoid great risks: they have been often fatal to youth, and have deformed their persons for the remainder of their lives, and have sometimes occasioned premature deaths.

4. Bows and arrows have caused frequent accidents; throwing stones is a very dangerous practice, and must be avoided: moderate exercise is healthful, but violent exercise should always be carefully guarded against.

5. Never join in a party to do mischief, nor associate with those who torment dumb creatures by way of sport.

6. Too many children, either from want of thought, or from improper example, are often disposed to be cruel. Our amiable moral poet, Cowper, says,

> I would not enter on my list of friends,
> Though grac'd with polish'd manners
> And fine sense, yet wanting sensibility,
> The man who needlessly sets foot upon a worm.

Refrain then from all acts of wanton cruelty: injure nothing that has life; for depend upon it the smallest creature possessed of life, can feel as well as you can.

7. Besides, what pleasure can you take in giving pain? To feel gratified at the sight of animals in anguish, writhing in misery, is a symptom of a malevolent disposition, and discovers a wicked heart.

8. To maim and torture flies, bees, and other insects, is as much an act of cruelty, as if done to larger animals. "The beetle you tread upon feels as much bodily anguish as when a giant dies." Therefore treat not the meanest insect with wanton cruelty.

9. Be always willing to oblige, and ever ready to assist your companions even though it may occasion you some trouble; and be not hasty to take offence at any one.

10. We all stand in need of the assistance of each other: "the race is not always to the swift, nor

the battle to the strong:" the rich cannot do without the services of the poor, nor the learned without the aid of the illiterate. To oblige others then is not only our duty but our interest, since by assisting others we gain assistance in return, and life being full of changes, we may soon need the help we now afford, and the favour we do to-day may be returned at some distant period. Thus interest binds the selfish to acts of kindness; but the truly liberal mind is influenced by superior and more generous motives.

11. Should any one use you unkindly; by no means retaliate, but rather refrain from his company.

12. Avoid all quarrels and the occasion of them; for quarrelling and fighting are the occupations of blackguards and prize fighters.

13. Some young persons are naturally kind and obliging, and seem to diffuse pleasure around them, others are quarrelsome and wish to be thought courageous: but they are mistaken in their notions; true courage is not exhibited by

boasting, insolence, fool-hardiness and cruelty.
Boasters are seldom truly brave, fool-hardiness
and violence indicate weakness of mind,
and cruelty is allied to cowardice. Noble and
generous minds neither resent nor even notice
trifles–they have learnt to forgive an injury and
to return good for evil.

14. If you notice any of your playfellows doing what
is wrong, reprove them mildly; and should they
at any time use improper words, shew your
disapprobation by telling them you must leave
them, if they do not desist: but never imitate
them; and on no account associate with boys
who are in the habit of using wicked and indecent language.

15. Be not arrogant on account of your birth or the
affluence of your parents; but shew a proper
respect to boys who are older than you, and
whose talents and proficiency in learning are
superior to your own.

16. Fret not at the playful jests of your companions,

though they sometimes fall smartly on you;
but jest with them again; yet always in good
humour, and with good manners.

17. Reflect not on any one's dress; much less on the
poverty and misfortunes of his friends, or on his
or their bodily imperfections.

18. Behave with the most scrupulous honour and
honesty in all your transactions with your companions; for honesty is always the best policy,
and is shewn as much in trifles as in greater
matters, in marbles as in sovereigns or bank
notes: cheating never prospers, you will always
lose by it in the end.

19. Be generous but not profuse: give freely whatever you can spare; but be care ful of what you
are likely to want for your own use.

20. Interrupt no one when engaged in business, or
attending to his studies; but wait till he is quite
at leisure to accompany you.

21. Join not in any dirty or forbidden diversions:
call no one by a reproachful name; never use a

disgraceful epithet, and laugh not unseasonably at your companions, much less at strangers.

22. On no occasion speak ill of the absent, and should others speak ill of them, unite not with them, but rather defend them, at least say all the good you can of them, or be silent.

23. What has occurred at school you have been taught never to relate out of it, nor should you ever repeat the conversation of your companions, particularly if likely to breed mischief; and tell not to any one what you have heard in your own or any other family.

II. CONDUCT
WHEN IN COMPANY WITH MEN

1. What has been said to you with respect to your behaviour to superiors is applicable to your conduct when in company with men; for men are certainly superior to boys, since years afford experience.

2. If then you are bound by the rules of good manners to treat your play-fellows with respect, it is still more imperative on you to deport yourself respectfully to persons of maturer years.

3. Aged persons are entitled to still more particular respect. Grey hairs are honourable if the behaviour suits. "The hoary head is a crown of glory" says the wise man, "if found in the way of righteousness."

4. The Lacedemonians are famed for the respect they paid to the aged. It is recorded, that an old man going late to the theatre at Athens, found it crowded on his arrival, and no one had the civility to offer him a seat. On the contrary the Athenians ridiculed his embarrassment, till quite out of countenance, the old man took refuge in that part of the theatre in which the Spartan ambassadors were sitting, who instantly rose and gave him the most honourable place. This act which the Athenians had not the

virtue to perform, they had still the good sense to applaud.

5. It is really disgusting to hear a rude boy answer an aged man with flippant pertness; it is quite shocking to see a saucy stripling treat a person old enough to be his grandfather with familiarity and disrespect. Reverence then the hoary head, and pay the utmost respect and attention to persons in advanced years.

6. Be not forward to speak when in the company of men: too great forwardness is very unseemly in young persons; wait till you are spoken to, then rise and answer with proper respect.

7. Wait the remarks of the person who addresses you, in good temper; should he contradict you, presume not to argue with him, for more years have given him an opportunity of being wiser than yourself.

8. Should you think a man mistaken in any thing he states to the company, do not attempt to correct him; if you are convinced he is wrong

do not presume to contradict him; leave this to some one who has more years and experience than you have.

9. Should a foolish thought be uttered in company, or any indecent word spoken, (for all men are not persons of sense and virtue,) let not your looks show that you either take notice of it, or understand it.

10. Be not forward in talking of trifles relating to your boyish exploits, or of telling what silly boys of your acquaintance have said and done.

11. Speak of such things only as you comprehend, and of them with modesty and diffidence.

12. If you happen to be at too great distance from a person who speaks to you, go nearer, but not close to him, before you answer; and reply to any thing that is said to you without repeating the identical words.

13. Let modesty, humility, and diffidence mark your conduct in all companies, but particularly when you are in company with men; and let it

be repeated and deeply impressed upon you,
that you will generally get more good and gain
greater credit by listening, than by talking.

PART V

ATTITUDE, &c.

———◆•◆•◆———

I. INTRODUCTORY REMARKS

1. To give directions with respect to attitude, may be thought an invasion of the province of the dancing master: a few remarks however may be useful to such as have not the advantage of one.

2. There is a certain mien and motion of the body, and its parts, both in acting and speaking, which are very graceful and pleasing.

3. These consist in the proportion and harmony between every one's person and condition; in confidence opposed to sheepish bashfulness; and in avoiding all affectation and singularity.

4. Young men, for example, should be active and sprightly, not mimical and restless: grave men

should be slow and deliberate, not dull and
sluggish.

5. Some persons know not how to look, speak, or
move, for fear of doing amiss, but always blush
and are not able to bear the least chiding, a
harsh word, or angry look, without being affected beyond measure.

6. Whatever is according to nature is best: what is
contrary to it is always distasteful, and betrays
vanity and indiscretion.

7. Nothing is graceful but what is our own, either
naturally or by adoption: you should therefore
endeavour to do every thing freely and easily;
then your efforts will appear to be dictated by
nature, or to proceed from a graceful habit.

8. Constraint undervalues an action, as does the
seeming to do every thing with a studied design;
yet still worse than this is an affectation of
negligence.

II. STANDING

1. To attain a graceful manner in moving, it is first necessary to learn how to stand firm and still: for this purpose hold up your head; as on this depends all grace in standing or in motion.

2. While the head is erect, let it remain free and easy: to be stiff is almost as bad as to stoop.

3. Your head being held up in an easy, graceful manner keeps the whole body erect; whereas if you poke your head forward, you will at the same time thrust out your back, and appear like a person with a distorted spine.

4. When you can hold your head upright and at ease, and you have learnt to stand without stooping, observe carefully how you place your feet, and how you dispose of your hands.

5. You must turn your feet outwards, for that will enable you to stand firmly, and with ease and gracefulness, while a person who turns his feet inwards, stands as if he were about to fall.

6. Place your feet at a small distance from each other, not too close, nor yet too far asunder.

7. Thrust not your hands into your small clothes; nor into any of your pockets; nor place your arms across, nor fold them over your breast as some vulgar boys do.

8. Put your right hand into your waistcoat, about three buttons from the bottom, and let your left hand hang gracefully down by your side.

III. WALKING, SALUTING, PASSING, MAKING A BOW, &c.

1. Be not negligent even of your walk; but try to walk gracefully; endeavour to acquire an easy, firm, and manly carriage. A clumsy, mean walk is very disgusting, and betrays a low education. Avoid a heavy, lazy gait; a hurrying, shuffling gait; and a proud, affected gait.

2. In walking hold up your head, as you have been directed to do in standing; and keep your body

erect; tread firmly and place your hands in an easy and graceful position.

3. Do not swing your hands and arms about as you walk; but let them fall at ease; do not lift your leg too high; and mind and bring it down with your knee straight; this will naturally raise the other.

4. To bow to any one passing, raise your right hand gracefully to your hat, put your fore-finger as far as the crown with your thumb under the brim, then raise your hat gently, look at the person to whom you bow, and bend your body slowly forward, hold your left hand down by your side, neither drawing it backward nor forward; if the person be on the right side, move the right leg; if on the left side move the left, keeping the other leg firm; let your body be bowed moderately, not extravagantly.

5. To make a bow, take off your hat as above directed and bring it down to your knee: see that the inside of your hat fronts the person to whom you bow, and let your hand fall straight down;

bring both your arms a little forward, and bow your head and body together; as you cast your eyes upon the person to whom you are bowing; when you begin to touch your hat, incline them a little downwards; bend your left leg a little to assist the right when making your bow. When you have bowed, rest upon the leg which is placed foremost, draw up your body a little, then gracefully raise your hat to your head.

IV. TAKING LEAVE, OFFERING OR RECEIVING ANY THING

1. When you are about to retire from any company, rise slowly and gracefully from your seat, and take your hat.
2. Stand till the company perceive you are about to depart, with your left hand at ease in your waistcoat, and your hat in the other: let your right hand fall straight down that your hat may hang as low as your knee.

3. In this posture address your eyes modestly to the principal person in company and bow retiring; make a general bow to the rest of the company.
4. Keep your feet at a little distance from each other, and bow inclining your eyes a little downward: preserve the right knee straight, and let the left rest upon the fore part of the foot, that the heel may not touch the ground: then drawing this leg gently back, the heel will come to the ground, after which recover firmly on that heel and draw your body upwards; let your body rise with care; and look upwards as you raise your head.
5. Be not too profuse of your bows; for too much ceremony is ridiculous.
6. Whatever you give or receive, take it in your right hand; and bow your head and body gently forward, as you present any thing.
7. When you have delivered it, draw your arm back gently, and let it fall with ease into its proper

place. When any thing is offered to you, receive it in the same way and retire as above directed.

V. MISCELLANEOUS REMARKS, AND CONCLUSION

1. To endeavour to please those with whom you are connected, and indeed all with whom you have any intercourse, is a most laudable pursuit, and particularly deserving the attention of young persons. A fixed and habitual resolution of thus endeavouring to please, is a circumstance which will seldom fail of effect, and its effect will every day become more visible as this habit increases in strength.
2. This resolution must be regulated by a very considerable degree of good sense.
3. It is a maxim of almost general application that what pleases us in another will also please others in us.
4. A constant and habitual attention to the

different dispositions of mankind, to their ruling passions, and to their peculiar or occasional humours, is absolutely necessary.

5. A person who would please must possess a firm, equal and steady temper, and an easy and graceful manner; as distant from bashfulness on the one hand, as from impudence on the other.

6. He who thinks himself sure of pleasing, and he who despairs of it, are equally sure to fail. The one by his assuming vanity, is inattentive to the means of pleasing; and the other from fear is rendered incapable of employing them.

7. As then you wish to be loved and esteemed; as you desire to have your company sought and your conduct commended, learn to behave yourself well at all times, and on every occasion.

8. Good behaviour does not consist in excess of ceremony; for excess of ceremony shews want of breeding. That politeness is most genuine which excludes all superfluous formality.

9. Deference to others is the golden rule of

politeness as well as of morals, and has its seat in the heart. "Whatsoever you would that others should do unto you, do you even so to them."

10. This complaisance, this denying of self, this respect to the feelings of others, renders a superior amiable, an equal agreeable, and an inferior acceptable.

11. It is indeed much to be regretted that it should ever happen that persons possessing considerable mental qualifications, should ever be awkward in their manners, and ungainly in their deportment, yet this unfortunately is sometimes the case.

12. It is however by no means necessary that the cultivation and improvement of the mind should be neglected, that the exterior graces may be attended to. You may have just as much knowledge and learning when you behave civilly and politely as if you were rude and disagreeable.

13. It must then be a sad and ridiculous neglect to

omit a proper care of your person and manners; and indeed must prevent your usefulness in the world; for people will not half so readily follow good advice when obtruded in a rude manner from a rough exterior, as when given gracefully and with a polished address.

14. However the ungraceful may laugh at those exterior accomplishments which they do not possess, it is a fact that these accomplishments are of the greatest importance towards your gaining the approbation of mankind.

15. Your intimate friends and those who are thoroughly acquainted with you, may love and value you for the internal graces of the mind; but persons in general, who have merely a superficial knowledge of you can only judge by your appearance, and if that be pleasing and graceful, they will naturally like you better than if you were awkward and disgusting.

16. To pass through this world with any tolerable degree of comfort, and to gain the love of your

fellow creatures, it is quite necessary that you should at all times make it your study to please, and to the best of your ability, to help and assist all you meet with in need of assistance.

17. To put on a hypocritical appearance of love and affection where you do not feel it, is indeed a degree of vile meanness which every honest bosom must detest; but to win the esteem of all by a polite and easy behaviour, is no way repugnant either to sincerity or duty.

18. On the contrary, when by so doing you can render yourself more universally admired, and thereby your virtues more esteemed, it becomes a duty to cultivate those methods which are most likely to be attended with good effects.

19. Under the mistaken idea that it does not signify how they appear provided they are really good, some persons neglect all the little accomplishments so necessary to distinguish the gentleman from the clown, and thus their merits remain hidden under so thick a veil of

ungraceful awkwardness that one can scarcely give them credit for possessing any good qualities whatever.

20. The world at large is captivated by outward appearance, and generally bestows its smile or its frown according to exterior circumstances, and though a virtuous mind would by no means give up one duty, or comply even with the appearance of one vice to secure its approbation or avoid its displeasure; yet when its approbation may be purchased with perfect innocence, it is not only allowable, but very desirable to gain it, particularly as by so doing you are likely to become a more useful and efficient member of society.

21. The virtues themselves indeed appear far more brilliant attended by the graces, than when left destitute; and in the one case, all ranks and conditions will admire them; whereas in the other, they will be disregarded except by the wise and discerning few.

22. The greatest impediments however to good behaviour are ignorance, pride, envy, ill humour,
and ill nature.

23. An ignorant person is continually saying or
doing something that is sure to give pain to
some one. When he opens his mouth you may be
certain that he will blunder out some expression
or other, if not to make himself blush, yet which
will probably tinge the cheek of others. When
he does any thing it is generally in the most
awkward and ungraceful manner. He times
nothing properly, but does and says every thing
out of season and out of place.

24. A proud person is so inflated with his own
importance, that he is satisfied with nothing
short of continual homage. He is displeased if
not saluted in due order, mode and form, and
must always have the most honourable place
assigned him. He is exceedingly jealous of his
dignity, and every moment fancying himself
affronted. Yet the homage and honour which he

thus exacts, he pays with the utmost reluctance to others, though greatly his superiors.

25. An envious person is always miserable and constantly diffuses misery around him. He is the very pest of society. He exhales a tainted atmosphere. Whatever respect is paid to another person, he imagines is so much detracted from himself He cannot bear to look upon merit except through some dense medium, and then he acts like those philosophers who gaze at the sun for no other purpose than to enumerate his spots.

26. An ill-humoured person is seldom pleased with any thing long together. He is subject to perpetual vexations; the slightest circumstance excites his spleen; the most casual and trifling misadventure rouses his indignation. He is then, vexed with himself, vexed with his friends, and vexed with all around him. He frets and fumes and is constantly in a state of irritability; and like the troubled sea is seldom long at rest.

27. An ill-natured person so far from striving

to avoid giving any one pain, would be quite displeased with himself if he afforded any one pleasure. He would scarcely do a person a good turn even to promote his own interest; yet he would at any time go a mile out of his way to mar a person's mirth or cause him a vexation.

28. So long then as ignorance prevails, so long as these evil dispositions are indulged and cherished, all pretensions to genuine politeness are fallacious. It is true the veil of dissimulation may conceal them for a time, but they will soon burst through the flimsy covering and appear in all their native deformity.

29. This is a lesson which cannot be too frequently inculcated; our beneficent Creator intended that we should mutually contribute to each other's happiness; all therefore who by ill-temper, ill-nature, envy, pride, or any other bad passion become a trouble and uneasiness to those with whom they are connected, in a measure defeat this benevolent purpose, and are consequently

guilty of a great crime. Such persons, unless they repent and amend, must expect not only to lose the good will of mankind; but, what is of infinitely greater consequence, to forfeit the favour of Heaven.

30. Ill-nature indeed tends to no good purpose, on the contrary, it leads to numberless bad ones, and lays the foundation of much wretchedness and woe. There never was an instance perhaps of a person being happy who permitted himself to be ill-tempered to others.

31. Indeed happiness and ill-temper cannot exist together. No one can possibly feel comfortable while all about him are uneasy and dislike his company; and no one can like the society of him who is always morose and ill-humoured.

32. The heart that suffers itself to be agitated by spleen or ill-nature can find no consolation to abate its anguish; its sufferings arise wholly from itself, it must therefore always carry its wretchedness along with it.

33. Consider the dreadful consequences of ill-temper; it is a sin whose evil effects spread through whole families; it greatly interrupts the happiness of all with whom it has any intercourse, as well as utterly destroys all peace in the bosom of its unhappy possessor.

34. Guard against it then, with all the care you would guard against some deadly serpent, the slightest touch from whose fangs would prove fatal; and never on any account allow yourself to be sullen or out of humour.

35. One powerful inducement for you to cultivate the art of pleasing when young is that in spite of your utmost care, old age will destroy and obliterate those exterior graces which in youth appear so engaging. You ought therefore diligently to cultivate that good humour and that sweetness of manners which will counterbalance every deformity, and which will make your company and conversation still please, when every outward beauty and natural grace have forsaken you.

36. The company of old people in general is far from being agreeable to the young and lively; one reason for which is, that in the days of their youth they were not careful enough to acquire that goodness of temper which alone can make them pleasing in the decline of life.

37. Good-humour to be of any value must be a settled disposition of the mind; not merely a sudden fit which discovers itself on particular occasions, or when it happens to be pleased.

38. The sourest and most morose person upon earth will sometimes be calm and good humoured, when nothing contradicts his fancy; but such good humour is liable to be blown away upon the first disappointment or contradiction, and is not deserving of the smallest regard, or worthy of being called a virtue.

39. But persons who maintain a constant sweetness of temper, not only when events conspire to please, but when things happen cross and vexatious, are certainly entitled to our love and admiration.

40. Endeavour then while you are young and in health and spirits to conquer your inclinations, and learn to conform to the will of others; for depend upon it when you grow old and labour under the pains and infirmities attendant upon age, it will be too late to improve the temper, or to correct an untoward disposition.

41. Above all things earnestly implore the assistance of Divine Grace to enable you to subdue those evil propensities; and let this truth be deeply impressed on your mind, that "he is more a hero who by divine help conquers himself, than he who subdues the best fortified city."

CONCLUSION

To conclude, in the words of Dr. Ash, "there is nothing that contributes more to good manners than a good mind. If you have no ill designs to accomplish, no mean and selfish passions to gratify; if you are contented, cheerful, and good tempered; if you discover in all your behaviour that you really wish well to all about you, and do as much as is in your power to make every one as happy as yourself, though you should be deficient in some little punctilios, you are sure to gain the good will of all your acquaintance. But on the other hand, should you be really wicked and designing, should you be ready to take all advantages of the vanity or necessity of your neighbours, be void of pity and compassion; and in short, love no one, nor care for any one, but yourself; though you should be ever so well-bred, perfectly understand all the modes of civility, and practise them with all imaginable address, put on the fairest outside upon all occasions, and exceed every one in the art of pleasing, you will soon be known, and when known, depend upon it, you will be despised and abandoned by all mankind."

FINIS